In this book, we're going to talk about some of the most famous entrepreneurs of all time. So, let's get right to it!

WHAT IS AN ENTREPRENEUR?

An entrepreneur is a person who comes up with a vision for a business and then takes action to create that business. There is a great deal of risk when a businessperson begins a business, but sometimes it can bring great profits and many other types of rewards as well.

THE MOST FAMOUS ENTREPRENEURS OF ALL TIME

Biography Book 3rd Grade
Children's Biographies

Speedy Publishing LLC
40 E. Main St. #1156
Newark, DE 19711
www.speedypublishing.com

An Entrepreneur

Throughout history there have been many famous entrepreneurs. Here are a few profiles of the many successful entrepreneurs that have influenced American culture.

Andrew Carnegie

Andrew Carnegie

(1835-1919)

When Carnegie was only 18 years of age he began working for a railroad company as a telegraph operator. He was a hard worker and over time he became a superintendent.

He soaked up as much knowledge as he could and learned a great deal about how to run a business and how to invest.

Andrew Carnegie laying of the foundation stone of Waterford Free Library

This knowledge would pay off when he became an entrepreneur. He began to invest the money he made into oil, iron, and the construction of bridges.

In 1865, he started his first company, which was called the Keystone Bridge Company. Using his connections in the railroad business, he began to construct bridges and offer railroad ties for sale.

Eventually, Carnegie saw that steel was the material that would offer better results than iron for future building projects.

He created the Carnegie Steel Company and soon his company was the largest manufacturer of steel worldwide. In 1901, along with J.P. Morgan, who was a famous banker, he began a new company called U.S. Steel. He became one of the wealthiest men in the world and gave much of his fortune away to important causes, such as libraries and other educational institutions.

U.S. Steel Plant

John D. Rockefeller

John D. Rockefeller

(1839-1937)

When Rockefeller was 16 years old, he began working as a bookkeeper. He was very good with accounting and money and by the age of 20 he decided he wanted to start his own business.

He and a friend named Maurice Clark began selling produce and their new business made a profit in its first year. In 1863, Rockefeller saw an opportunity he could capitalize on.

At that time, whale oil was used for lamps, but it was getting more expensive to obtain and whales were becoming overhunted. He invested in kerosene.

Kerosene was created in refineries from oil that was drilled from under the Earth's surface. Clark was his partner in this new business and they did well. Eventually, Rockefeller bought out his partner.

Mining of oil shale

In 1870, Rockefeller created a new company called Standard Oil. He had a huge goal. He wanted to have complete control over all the world's oil because he knew it would make him a fortune.

As Rockefeller started to buy up his competitors one by one, his business became a monopoly, which simply means they controlled all aspects of the oil business.

Rockefeller and his son John Jr. in 1915

Around 1911, the United States government forced him to divide up his companies so other competitors would have a chance. By 1916, Rockefeller was the first billionaire on Earth. Today, the fortune he amassed would be worth about $350 billion. Rockefeller, like Carnegie, gave much of his fortune, over half a billion dollars, away before he died.

Thomas Edison

(1847-1931)

Edison started his first business when he was very young. He sold candy and newspapers on the railways. Then, one day his life changed when he saved the life of a child. The child had been running on the train tracks and was almost killed by a runaway train. The father of the child wanted to repay Edison for saving his son, so he began to train him to operate a telegraph.

Thomas Alva Edison

This was the beginning of Edison's interest in communications. Despite his lack of a formal education, Edison became a great inventor and filed for more than 1,000 patents during his lifetime.

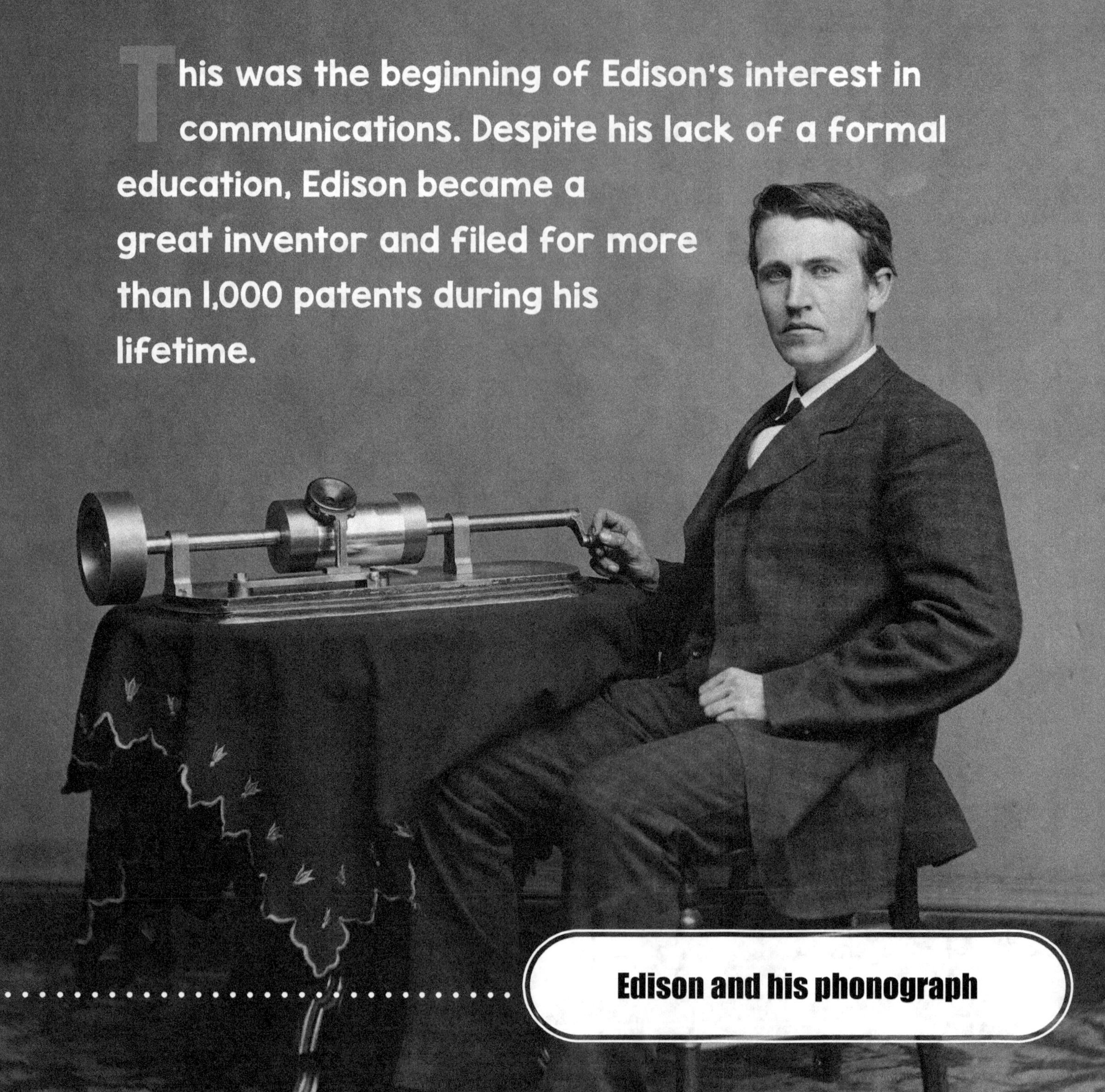

Edison and his phonograph

Edison's Menlo Park Laboratory, Michigan

He began a research laboratory in the city of Menlo Park in New Jersey, where he worked with a team to research and develop his ideas.

Edison had many different businesses in his lifetime, but perhaps the most famous was the Edison General Electric Company, which became the basis for the company General Electric, which is still in existence. Edison's inventions like the phonograph, the first practical light bulb powered by electricity, and the motion-picture camera still have a major impact on us today.

A portrait of Thomas Edison

Milton Hershey

(1857-1945)

When Hershey was very young he became a printing apprentice but he didn't like the work and he complained to his mother. She found him a job as a candy-making apprentice. He loved making candy and he knew he wanted this line of work to be his profession.

He was just nineteen years old when he started his first candy shop. He had lots of different types of candy and he worked extremely hard

but he ran out of funds and had to close down. He moved and went to work for another candy maker.

Later he opened another candy shop but that one didn't survive either. However, Hershey was persistent and didn't give up.

cararmel

For his third business, he decided to focus only on creating the best caramels. This third business finally reaped the rewards he was looking for. It became very successful. In fact, it was so successful that he eventually sold it for 1 million dollars.

chocolate bar

Then, Hershey had another innovative idea. He wanted to create a chocolate bar that was so affordable that even kids could buy it. He decided that he wanted to build a factory in the countryside of Pennsylvania. People thought he was crazy.

Who would come all the way out to the country to work in the Hershey chocolate factory? But, Milton Hershey didn't see that as a problem. He decided to build a town called Hershey in Pennsylvania so his employees would have a place to live. Today, the Hershey Company still makes delicious chocolate bars at an affordable price.

Hershey Factory, Penselvania

Henry Ford

(1863-1947)

Even though Ford's family were farmers, he was much more interested in machines than farming. At sixteen years of age, Henry Ford traveled to Detroit and became an apprentice to begin a career as a machinist. Ford didn't invent the automobile, but his first car design for the Model T Ford was innovative, because he produced it at a price that the everyday American could afford.

Henry Ford

Henry Ford Looking at V-8 engine

Eventually, over 15 million of these cars were sold and around 1918 over half the cars on American roads were Fords. Ford continued to perfect his car designs throughout the years and the Ford Motor

Company is still around today. Ford also created and perfected the assembly line process used throughout manufacturing industries around the world.

Walt Disney

(1901-1966)

Just like Carnegie and Edison, Walt Disney worked on the railways as a boy. He sold snacks as well as newspapers and he loved trains for the rest of his life. His other fascination was drawing. Walt loved to draw. Walt was too young to fight in World War I, but he went to France and drove Red Cross ambulances.

Walt Disney visited Dr. Werhner von Braun

Walt Disney and his wife

When he came back to America, he got a job at a studio that created art and later he created art for advertising. During these early years of his career, he met Ubbe Iwerks, an artist who had a lot of talent and was interested in the early field of cartoon animation. They became fast friends.

Walt had a big dream. He wanted to have his own business creating and selling animated cartoons. Along with his pal Ubbe, he started this company and called it Laugh-O-Gram.

The cartoons were quite popular, but they weren't making enough profit and the company went bankrupt. However, Walt wasn't going to let his dream die so easily.

Disney Land, Shanghai

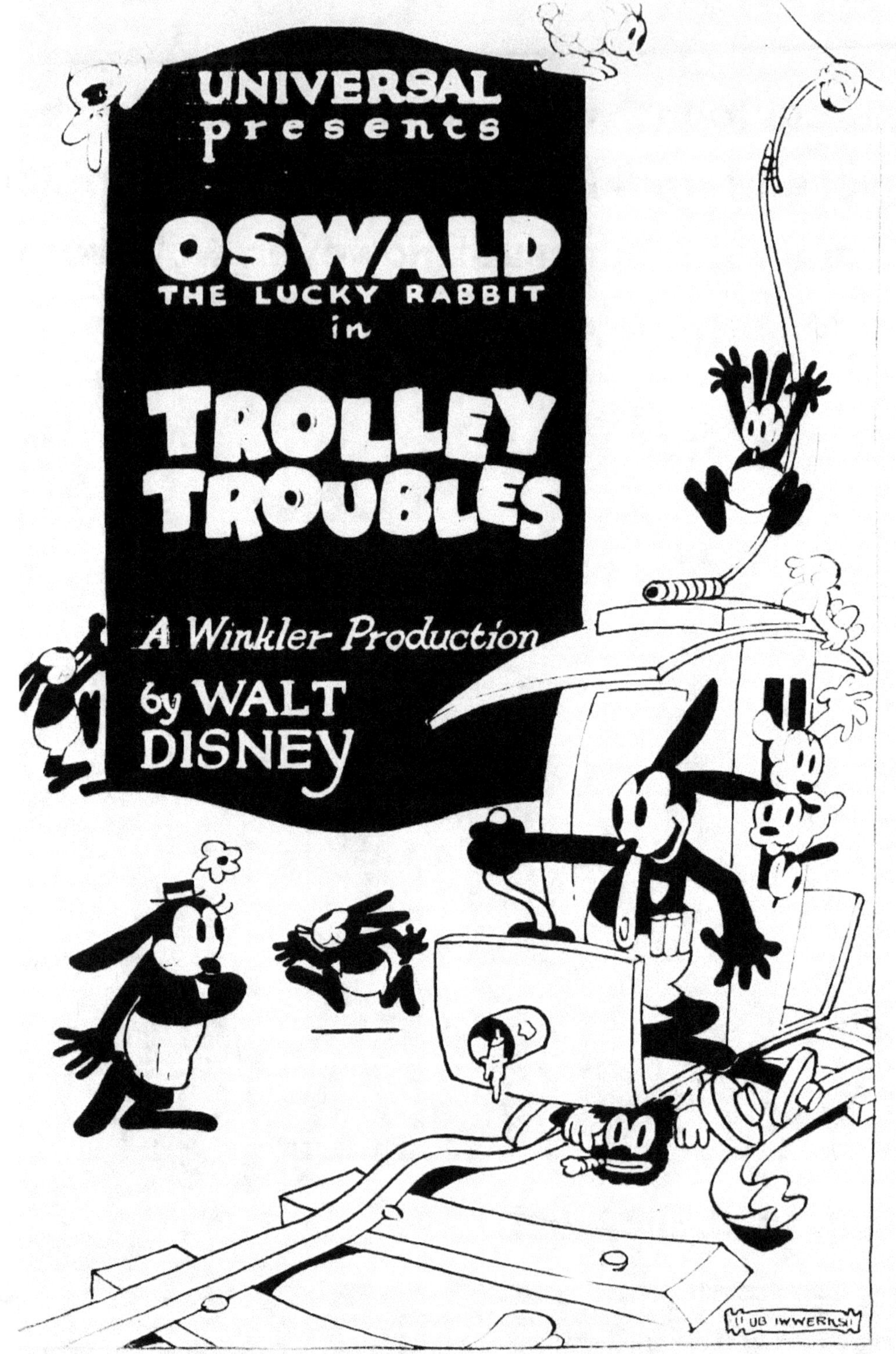
UNIVERSAL
presents
OSWALD
THE LUCKY RABBIT
in
TROLLEY
TROUBLES
A Winkler Production
by WALT
DISNEY
UB IWWERKS

He started over again in 1923, when he and his brother Roy launched a new studio and named it "Disney Brothers" after themselves. They created a new character called Oswald, who was a very funny rabbit. The Oswald cartoons were very successful and through a variety of unfortunate circumstances, Universal Studios got control of the rights to Oswald.

They also persuaded almost all of Walt's animators to leave and come to Universal. Only his friend Ubbe remained with Walt. After all this success, Walt had to start all over again. Walt worked with Ubbe to create their next character, Mickey Mouse. Building on the success of Mickey Mouse's cartoons, Walt decided that he wanted to create full-length films that were animated.

No one had ever done this successfully before and many people thought he was crazy. His first full-length animation was the movie Snow White and the Seven Dwarfs, which took five years to create, but was a huge success.

Many other full-length animated films followed and most of them were very successful. Eventually, Walt created huge theme parks to highlight the many beloved characters he featured in his films.

SUMMARY

An entrepreneur is someone who has a dream and creates a business from that dream. Most successful entrepreneurs have some traits in common. They are not afraid of calculated risks or failure. They view every defeat as a learning opportunity. They continue to persist even after they have gone bankrupt, sometimes many times. They work hard and they work smart. They know that in order to be winners they have to lead others and stay ahead of the competition with innovative ideas and products.

ENTREPRENEUR

Awesome! Now that you've read about some of the most famous American entrepreneurs, you may want to read more details about the life of Walt Disney, in the Baby Professor book Did Walt Disney Have His Happily Ever After? Biography for Kids 9-12 | Children's United States Biographies.

Visit
BABY PROFESSOR
EDUCATION KIDS
www.BabyProfessorBooks.com
to download Free Baby Professor eBooks
and view our catalog of new and exciting
Children's Books

www.ingramcontent.com/pod-product-compliance
Lightning Source LLC
LaVergne TN
LVHW060828170826
845678LV00010B/1929

* 9 7 9 8 8 6 9 4 3 7 1 2 9 *